Does Christianity Make Sense?

Mike Phillips

While this book is designed for the reader's personal enjoyment and profit, it is also intended for group study. A leader's guide is available from your local bookstore or from the publisher at $.75.

VICTOR BOOKS

a division of SP Publications, Inc., Wheaton, Illinois

Offices also in Fullerton, California • Whitby, Ontario, Canada • London, England

Scripture quotations are from the *New American Standard Bible* (NASB) © 1960, 1962, 1963, 1968, 1971, 1972, 1973. The Lockman Foundation, La Habra, California. Used by permission.

Quotations reprinted with permission of Macmillan Publishing Co., Inc. from *Mere Christianity* by C. S. Lewis. Copyright 1943, 1945, 1952. Pages 33, 39, 41, 125, 153-155, and 175. Other quotations taken from *The God Who Is There* by Francis A. Schaeffer. Copyright 1968 by L'Abri Fellowship, Switzerland, and used by permission of InterVarsity Press; *The Church at the End of the 20th Century* by Francis A. Schaeffer. Copyright by L'Abri Fellowship, Switzerland, and used by permission of InterVarsity Press.

Library of Congress Catalog Card Number: 77-092292
ISBN: 0-88207-513-6

© 1978 by SP Publications, Inc.
World rights reserved
Printed in the United States of America

VICTOR BOOKS
A division of SP Publications, Inc.
P.O. Box 1825 • Wheaton, Ill. 60187

Dedicated to
Clarry, Don, Mark,
and to George

Contents

1

We Take a Lot
for Granted

I was going to begin with a clever anecdote. I thought I would grab your attention and entice you into thinking, "Ah, this is going to be an enjoyable book. I'll keep reading."

But I chose not to do that; and I'll tell you why.

This is a book about ideas; about how you and I think. A philosophy book, if you will. Of course, I hope it will be much simpler than what we've always thought philosophy to be. And more useful too.

But no matter how simple you make them, there are certain things in life that require a good deal of effort to understand. And certainly the things we'll be talking about—thoughts, ideas, beliefs—are like that. If you want to understand these things, it is just no good expecting answers to come automatically. They won't. If you want to understand the way you think and why you believe, there comes a time when you've simply got to say, "I know it means work, but I'm going to dig in and get hold of these ideas."

Why go into this? Because I want you to understand what kind of book this is. It is a book about ideas. Though it will be as simple as I can make it, you will not be able to read this book (and get much out of it) without some concentrated thinking.

So if this doesn't interest you, and if serious and thoughtful reading is not your style, then I suggest you go no further.

Why Do We Think the Way We Do?

If you are still with me, let's begin with the question, "Why do we think the way we do?"

"That's too big a question," you say. "Narrow it down a bit. What exactly do you mean?"

You're right. It is too broad, so let's back up a little. Is it even possible to ask a question like that? Can we really know why we think a certain way? Do we have any basis for an answer?

Well, I think we do. But to discover anything about why we think, we need to go back further still—to the very beginnings of our lives. From the moment you and I were born, we have been influenced by our parents, our teachers, our friends, and many others. Through them, many basic ideas and assumptions about life have slowly become part of us, without our even knowing it. Our minds have simply absorbed these things. We haven't asked for proof, but have just taken them for granted.

This is natural. It happens to us all. There is nothing wrong with it. In fact, it is necessary. Without these basic assumptions about life we would have no foundation from which to learn and grow. We need these suppositions to progress in our thinking.

But the thing to notice is that we don't reason out these assumptions or try to prove them. We take them for granted. So this whole process usually has taken place without our being aware of it. We have come into these basic assumptions about life more or less automatically. There are a number of words we might use to describe these basic assumptions that undergird everything we think and do from day to day—suppositions, postulates, presumptions, presuppositions.

But all these words mean pretty much the same thing: ideas and ground rules about life we have come to accept as true without asking for proof. We have taken them for granted. They have become part of our very being.

In mathematics these assumptions are called postulates. They are assumed true right off the bat, before you do anything else. All mathematics is based on these postulates.

In the same way, our lives are based on our own assumptions. What we do, how we think and reason, the way we relate to people and situations —all these things have their roots in our presuppositions about life. These are our rock-bottom basics. Our later beliefs are formed on the basis of these presuppositions.

Most of the things I take for granted are obvious. I don't even think about them. When I go to bed I know my body needs rest. I don't consciously have to make that decision every night.

When I flip on a light switch I don't stop to wonder, "Will the light go on?" I take that for granted because it has switched on in the past.

One child grows up valuing an education. Another thinks it is a waste of time. One man believes in hard work as one of the keys to a meaningful life. Another tries to do as little as he can. They have had different influences and therefore have acquired different presuppositions about the value of school and work.

So though our assumptions differ widely, we all have them. You and I may have completely different ideas on something we talk about. But we both operate on the basis of certain things we hold to be basic.

These assumptions you and I take for granted, our presuppositions, are the bases for why we think as we do.

An Important Assumption

Francis Schaeffer, noted writer and speaker, has pointed out in one of his books, *The God Who Is There* (Downers Grove, Illinois, InterVarsity Press, 1968, Chap. 1), that there is one very important assumption in life that used to be held in common by nearly everyone. Until a relatively short time ago, nearly all men, whether they had ever analyzed it or not, took for granted that right and wrong, truth and falsehood existed. They were absolutes. Right and wrong were different and could never be mingled. Truth and falsehood could never apply to the same statement. They were different.

A belief in absolutes implied an equal belief in opposites. If a thing was true, its opposite was false. This one presupposition was the basis for all men's thought and talk among themselves. If one thing was right, then its opposite had to be wrong. If something was true, then the opposite had to be false.

If you and I had been playing baseball and I hit a foul ball, it would have been foul. I wouldn't have said, "No, it's fair!" It couldn't have been both fair and foul at the same time.

That's what I mean by absolutes. It had to be one or the other. You couldn't have both right and wrong, truth and falsehood, foul and fair at the same time. They were opposite.

"That's obvious," you may say, "not even worth saying."

If you'd been living a hundred years ago you'd be right. It would have been obvious. (But let's continue on a little further.) Not only did men believe that right and wrong, truth and falsehood existed in specific instances; they also believed that in the final analysis you could point to some standard and say, "This is *always* right, this is *absolute* truth."

Of course, men all through history have differed strongly on what specific things were right and wrong. By saying they believed in an "absolute truth" I don't mean they all agreed on what that was. They didn't. Men have always argued heatedly over what was right and what was wrong. But they did agree on one point—there was a difference. And this is the key—right and wrong, truth and falsehood, were different. You could not just do anything you liked.

So you and I could have sat down and discussed right and wrong. We might have disagreed, but we would both have been taking for granted that right and wrong existed. I might have said, "A is right, B is wrong."

You might have then said, "No, B is right and A is wrong."

But neither of us would have said, "They are both right." Though there was disagreement, we would both have been assuming that right and wrong were different.

During the Reformation, the Catholic Church said, "We are right, Luther is wrong," while Luther said, "I am right, the Church is wrong."

But neither of them said, "We are both right, it just depends on how you look at it."

And as recently as the Second World War this can be seen. The Allies of the West did not fight the German army merely because they happened to disagree. They felt the Germans were wrong, according to some universal standard of absolute right and wrong. Therefore they had to be stopped.

Of course this went without saying. The presupposition that in some absolute way right was different from wrong was in effect in all areas of life. Everyone thought and reasoned on that basis.

Thinking men down through the ages have operated on this basis since man first became aware of himself and began to ask, "What does life mean?" Philosophers in every era have arrived at different answers to the basic questions of life. Some of their answers have been religious, others nonreligious, some psychological, some practical, some theoretical. But the thing to keep in mind is that all these philosophers believed such a thing as the truth could be found. They assumed answers existed to the basic questions of life, man, and the universe.

The same thing can be seen in the birth and development of science. Modern science arose out of a mentality which took rules, order, and absolute truth for granted. The early scientists assumed the universe to be governed by reason and order, so they knew they could discover its secrets. Because there was truth, there was a basis for knowledge. Answers could be found, if only research, insight, methods, and imagination could take them far enough. This is what motivated the early scientists from Galileo and Copernicus to Newton; answers could be found because the universe was based on absolutes.

Taking absolutes for granted pervaded every field. Art and music were based on orderly beauty because within a framework of absolute truth, there is order.

If an evangelist stood up to preach he could say, "This is true, believe it." Many of his listeners might have disagreed with him that it was true. But they would all have agreed that *if* it was in fact true, then certainly it was to be believed.

So discussion centered around what was true and what was not. You would rarely, however, have heard two people discussing whether such a thing as truth existed. They took that for granted. Although most men were unaware of it, this assumption that opposites were truly opposites and that truth and falsehood definitely existed, *and were different,* influenced their entire outlook on life.

2

The Theory
of Relativity

Now all this has changed. In every field, from philosophy to music to theology, there has been a shift in the way of looking at truth. The change has been gradual, and mostly unnoticeable, for those of us in the Western middle class. Many of the men who opened the doors to these changes did not realize what they were doing and were not even known by the majority of their peers. But the effect on our whole culture, and on you and me, has been overwhelming.

The roots of this change go back four hundred years, to the early days of the Reformation. But it has not really been until now, in our own generation, that the full impact has begun to be felt.

In a nutshell, the change can be described this way. Everyone used to take for granted there were absolutes (right and truth, which were opposite from wrong and falsehood). Most people today, however, assume there are none. Everything is relative (instead of absolute). I can only judge what is right for me. I can never know what is right, because "right" doesn't exist. The presupposition of modern man is: "There are no absolutes."

Though this may sound somewhat philosophical to you, the results of such an assumption are rather astounding. For we are now at the point where opposites are no longer defined as opposite. Right and wrong are not necessarily different. Truth and falsehood can be applied to the same statement. Everything is relative only to a certain person in a certain situation.

A hundred years ago you could have said to me, "God exists," and if I had believed you I would have had to conclude that "God does not exist" was a false statement.

Today however, you could say, "God exists," and someone else could come along and reply, "God may exist for you, but for me there is no God."

Now the remarkable thing is not that he made such a statement. The remarkable thing is that this statement is accepted as a perfectly legitimate opinion today. This person has just said, "God exists and God doesn't exist."

One hundred years ago he would have been laughed at. His statement would have seemed foolish. Yet today many people hardly lift an eyebrow. Two completely opposing claims in the same sentence are heard, and often accepted enthusiastically, because of the modern presupposition that everything is relative, and there are no absolutes.

You see examples of this around you daily. You see them without even thinking about them because modern thought patterns have so infiltrated your thinking. Divorce is another example. There was a time when divorce was wrong. That was that. But to the modern man, divorce is not wrong at all, in any final way. It is relative—sometimes right, sometimes wrong. It all depends on the individuals and circumstances involved.

Morality has been affected. Anything is right, if it is right for those involved. About marriage modern man says, "Marriage is fine if it is right for you. If not, then just live together for a while." Right and wrong no longer exist for him. They can only be discussed in relative terms.

We hardly notice this change. Yet it is all about us. It has crept in so slowly we haven't been aware of it. Yet how many times have we either found ourselves involved in, or hearing, a conversation like this, between two people visiting together for the first time in years.

"Oh Tricia! I haven't seen you for ages!"

"Ann! It's good to see you. What are you doing now?"

"Oh, I'm living with this guy for a while. It's good. We really like each other. We're just going to see what happens."

Now even though Tricia may have been raised in an environment that taught such an arrangement to be absolutely wrong, and though she still clings to much of that ethic herself, she may reply,

"That's really good. I'm glad you're so happy with each other."

The conversation might continue with Ann asking, "What about you?"

"Oh, I'm married and have two small children. My husband and I are very close, and we're excited about our family."

"That's really exciting. I'm happy for you."

And these two young women wouldn't simply be covering up their true feelings with pleasantries. I think their happiness for one another would be genuine. You see how the loss of absolutes has crept in? One hundred years ago such a conversation would have ended much differently. The two women were living lives that were diametrically opposed. They could not both be considered "right" or "exciting." If one of their lives was "good" then the other just couldn't be. They were opposite.

Not so today. Even though they are opposite life-styles, they could both be considered right for the persons involved. Opposites are no longer necessarily opposite. Absolutes, as a final standard of right and wrong, and truth and falsehood, no longer exist.

For the moment, I'm not passing judgment on any of this. I'm not saying it is good or bad. I'm simply trying to show what a tremendous shift in thinking has occurred. A few years ago you could have said to someone, "This is true," and he would have understood you. You would have been on his wavelength, so to speak. Not that he would have agreed. But you would have been understood. He would have known you also meant the opposite thing was false.

If I said, "Sex must be reserved for marriage,"

the person listening would have known I also meant, "Sex outside marriage is wrong."

But today it is different. You could get up and say, "Sex outside marriage is beautiful." I might then say, "Sex outside marriage is wrong." Still a third person might say, "Sex is always wrong, in or out of marriage."

Now it is clear all three statements contradict each other. Yet those listening could well applaud and say, "Yes. These men are all right. For them, in their circumstances, these statements are all true." No absolute truth. No absolute right or wrong.

The effects of this relative way of looking at everything are felt in all areas of life, particularly between parents, still trying to live under the old suppositions, and their children, growing up under the influence of these new trends where right and wrong are not universally taken for granted. In the past, my father could have said to me, "Be good." I might not have taken his advice, but I certainly would have known what he meant. We would both have agreed that "good" existed, though we may have argued about what exactly it consisted of.

Today, however, if I have accepted the modern presupposition of relativism, I may well view that statement from my father as nonsense. My total lack of response wouldn't mean that my standards of good and bad were different from those of my father. It would simply mean that to me, in my modern way of thinking, his message ("be good") was meaningless.

To the modern person living under relativism,

"good" has no real meaning. It is a relative thing. You can't talk about goodness and badness as such. You can only talk about them relative to a certain person. So in responding to my father's message, I would feel that whatever I chose to do was "right for me," and what he chose to do was "right for him." It wouldn't matter that the two choices were opposites. They could still both be "right."

So if good is no longer the opposite from bad, there is indeed no sense to the statement, "Be good." Anything is good, anything is right, as long as it suits me. There are no absolutes to judge by. Right and wrong can only be measured for each individual.

Looking at it in this way, the present generation of young adults and their parents are not just twenty or thirty years apart. They are hundreds of years apart. Because during the present generation, many hundreds of years of slow changes in the way we think have suddenly surfaced and made themselves felt.

One of the major results of this fading away of absolutes is evinced in the realm of the supernatural. Because man has always believed in absolute right and wrong, he has also always believed in a God or gods as the absolute right, the absolute truth. Of course, there have been as many notions about the nature and character of the supernatural as there have been men on the earth. This classic disagreement has probably influenced history more than any other single dispute. But despite disagreements over the nature of the supernatural, there was never a major dispute over whether or not it existed. That was something men took for granted.

But again, this has all changed. Although the trend had begun long before, a key step in swaying the general public to this change was the publication of Darwin's *Origin of Species* in the mid-1800s. The significant element in Darwin's theory was not evolution. It was what he said about the nature of the supernatural. Darwin stated, in effect, "Everything in the universe has come about by chance. There was no beginning or assistance from any sort of personal supernatural being. The evolutionary process has continued on from this impersonal beginning on the basis of sheer chance mutations. We exist now because of chance. Nothing else."

The effect of this was devastating. It was felt in all areas of life sooner or later. It was not long before the philosophers carried it a step further. They had already begun to move in this direction, but with Darwin's impersonal-chance theory to explain the beginning and development of life, they now said: "OK. If there is no personality, no absolute right, no absolute truth behind the universe, then ultimately, right and wrong have no meaning because there is no standard on which to base them. In the final outcome they are equal. There must be no definitive idea of "truth" because there is no absolute truth behind the universe. All is chance and impersonal." They concluded, "We will stop looking for absolute truth. We will only seek to find true meaning *for ourselves*. Even though two of us may arrive at opposite conclusions, we will be content."

So the philosophers stopped their search for ultimate answers.

And once the philosophers took the lead and opened the door, a reversal was felt in other pursuits as well. Modern art developed from the premise that absolutes, rules, and order were gone. An artist could paint a painting which to you or me might have looked like nothing but a mass of jumbled colors. But he could say, "Ah, this is really a portrayal of the meaning I have found in life." And because there were no longer any absolute standards on which to base a judgment, all we could say would be, "Oh, if that's what you meant it to be, then I guess for you that's what it is."

Now mind you, I'm not saying all modern art is ugly or that I don't like it. The point is that it shows us very clearly that absolute standards are no longer in effect. Everything is relative. Several hundred years ago there would have been some standard to judge a painting by. "This is a beautiful painting," would have been a meaningful statement.

Not so now. The only thing we can say is, "That is a beautiful painting *for you*." That's all that matters. Anything goes, as long as it has meaning for the artist.

The same thing has happened in music. Order, beat, rhythm, time, consistency, and pattern which had long been the standards for music began to be done away with. Music changed, and much of the orderliness left it. This did not begin with the modern and often chaotic rock music, but with many classics of the last century. Much of Debussy's music, though very beautiful, illustrates the abandonment of order as it has long been known in music. "Good, beautiful, meaningful" music became only what was good, beautiful, or meaningful to the composer.

I'm not judging recent music as bad or good. Much of it I enjoy. But these changes do show us once again how absolute standards have lost their meaning.

More recently, some theologians have taken up the same banner. Years ago they were most dogmatic and said, "If you don't agree with me, you're wrong."

But there's been a drastic change. Now they're saying, "It's OK if you don't agree with me, as long as what you believe gives your life meaning."

One person can say, "God doesn't exist. I'm my own man."

Another can say, "I find meaning for my life in loving others."

Another can say, "Jesus Christ is Lord of my life."

And still another can say, "Meaning for me is being good. Then in my next life I'll attain a higher level of consciousness."

And some theologians will say to them all, "That's good! You are all finding true meaning for yourselves."

A complete change! Absolute meaning is no more. Everything is relative to the individual. And once you accept relative presuppositions and agree to an impersonal beginning, it is impossible to cling to any definite belief in an Absolute Being.

So it is no surprise that only one hundred years after Darwin, some theologians began to say, "God is dead."

Now it does not really matter what our background has been. You may have been raised a Hindu, I may have been raised a Protestant, another an intellectual agnostic, another a Catholic, another nothing at all. Once any one of us accepts the basic assumption that no absolutes exist in life, we are left without hope of finding any final answers to meaning in our lives. (And remember we can drift into this assumption simply by conforming to the shift in attitudes that has taken place about us, without even thinking about it.) We are left on our own.

Of course modern, thinking man would say, "But you can find meaning *for yourself*. You can find significance *for yourself*."

But that's not ultimate meaning. I'm talking about final, definite, absolute meaning. And any person today who has allowed himself to be swept along by the relative and nonabsolute assumptions which are the basis for modern thinking, has no hope of ever finding any *final* meaning in his life.

This is the cause for much of the despair and lack of purpose found in the world today. It isn't simply that things are bad. We can endure that. But we cannot live without meaning.

And modern thinking has led us just to that point. If we assume that absolutes do not exist, then ultimate meaning in life is but a dream. We will always wake to find it isn't there.

3

But Does the Theory Hold Water?

Are you with me so far? I hope so. For most of man's history, he has believed certain things to be absolutely true and right. This belief was based on the assumption that right, wrong, truth, and falsehood existed.

In recent times, modern thinkers have come to the conclusion that right, wrong, truth, and falsehood are all relative to each individual. Absolute right, wrong, and truth don't exist. This developed because there has been a switch in the basic assumption about life—a shift from believing that absolutes exist, to the current belief that they do not.

Since modern man no longer believes that any absolutes exist, he has been left without hope of finding any final, significant meaning in his life. Two conclusions are forced on him: everything exists by chance, and nothing has final meaning.

On reaching this point, modern man is faced with an enormous dilemma: he cannot live consistently with his theory. For he must live in reality, and two areas of reality daily confront him and tell him there has to be meaning; the world can't possibly be a victim of chance.

These two areas are man, himself, and the world. Modern man must live with himself, and he must live in the world. And if he holds a theory he cannot live by, then certainly that doesn't speak well for his theory. That is what man now faces as he tries to live on the basis of his relative assumptions where all has come about by chance.

Man, What Is He?

One of the first things we notice about man is that he is rational. He thinks, and so is different from animals, plants, rocks, water, or air. He knows himself to be unique; he is aware of his significance. Schaffer, in his book *The Church at the End of the Twentieth Century* (Downers Grove: Inter-Varsity Press, p. 14), points out that according to modern archaeological findings, there is evidence that many thousands of years ago cavemen buried their dead in flower petals. Even at that primitive stage of development, man knew there was something special about himself. He knew he was more than nothing.

It is this difference, this uniqueness man feels about himself as rational, that makes him feel, love, learn, reason, and fear insignificance. It is evidence of personality. It suggests that there must be more to him than a mere collection of atoms.

But for the modern thinker, man has come about by chance. There is really no difference between man and a lizard in terms of ultimate and lasting significance. Chance developments have simply made them different, and neither has any special meaning over the other. Therefore modern man cannot explain this personality, this rationality, this peculiar quality which makes man uniquely a man —this longing for meaning and ultimate significance. According to his chance theory, these things don't exist.

Now what makes this doubly difficult for a modern thinker to cope with is a further evidence that there is more to man than a chance collection of atoms. Not only is there evidence for personality, when man looks within himself, he finds that he leans toward a universal standard of behavior. Yet, the modern thinker maintains that standards, especially concerning right and wrong, do not even exist. The only standard is what each chooses to have for himself.

Like it or not, we all feel that we ought to be nice, we ought to be fair, we ought to tell the truth. We can't squirm out of it. Though our presuppositions may deny that such absolute standards exist, still we feel them.

Whenever I am driving down the highway and see an accident I immediately feel two things. I feel an urge to stop and help. Yet I also feel a desire to drive on rather than involve myself. I also find within myself a third impulse which tells me I ought to obey the first urge I felt to stop and help. There is something pressing in on me. It is not just that I've learned I should do good things. That is actually the first thing I felt—the impulse to stop and help. It is something else. Sometimes I obey it, and sometimes I do not.

But I find it very interesting that it is there at all. It must be more than simply something learned. For I have learned both good and bad things through the years. And these learned things—good and bad—influence me too. But somehow there is always this standard of behavior which I cannot escape, telling me which of my various impulses I ought to obey.

And the really interesting thing is that modern thinkers, who say there are no standards, feel this standard too and act upon it. You may say, "Right and wrong do not exist. They are only relative to each individual."

But let's say you and I go to a concert together. It is crowded, but we finally find seats. When you have to get up for a moment I say, "I'll save your seat for you." But when you return you find I deliberately gave your seat to someone else, and you are annoyed.

You may say, "No absolute standard exists. Right and wrong do not exist in any uniform way for everyone." But can you live consistently on that basis? Wouldn't you be irritated with me for breaking my word—breaking the standard?

We all observe these two things in ourselves—first, personality, rationality, something uniquely "mannish"; and second, a standard of absolute behavior pressing in on us. This places us, as modern people, in a position of tension. A position where we cannot consistently live with our nonabsolute, relative assumptions about life. Our presuppositions bring us to the conclusion that our life has come about by chance and has no ultimate meaning. Yet we cannot consistently live as if this were true. We are divided men.

One moment we say, "Absolutes—right, wrong, significance, personality, and good—do not exist." But the very next moment we experience an urge compelling us to do "right," and reacting when someone does us "wrong."

If we are honest we cannot deny this. We cannot deny the personality and meaning we feel. Our very being, and all we are as persons, cry out against it.

The Universe We Live In

The universe speaks of order and meaning, beauty and predictability. Chance is certainly the last word we'd ever use to describe the functioning of the universe. The form and order of the universe speak of planning, imagination, thought, and infinite creativity. Everything in our experience confirms that such order can only come about by careful planning.

Yet against all reason and all experience, modern man clings to his belief that the universe has come about by chance. The presupposition that says "absolutes do not exist" runs contrary to everything man sees and experiences. Francis Schaeffer reported that at the Massachusetts Institute of Technology, not many years ago, high speed computers were programmed to answer this question on the basis of mathematical probability: "Beginning with chaos and chance, could the present complexity of the universe ever have come about?" The computer's answer was consistently an emphatic "No!" (*The Church at the End of the Twentieth Century*, p. 15)

Yet even against such odds, many of us still say, "Everything exists because of chance."

But the universe runs in as orderly a way as anything we know. Night follows day, season follows season, cycle follows cycle. The universe, like a well-oiled machine, has been running smoothly for hundreds of centuries. Changes brought about by earthquakes and floods happen within the orderly whole. This is its beauty—the constant change yet the orderly dependability.

Everytime he gets caught up in the sights and sounds and smells of a warm evening at sunset, modern man is trapped in a dilemma between what he says—that all about him is nothing but chance with no meaning—and what he sees and feels within himself. He feels meaning, though he may deny it. He is uplifted by the beauty and the creativity of the world, though if pinned down, he would probably try to say there was no such thing as ultimate creativity. He is a man in tension—torn between what he sees and feels, and what he believes because of the assumptions he has made.

Many people today are not sure the external world is even there. "It is all an illusion," they say. Yet when they have a true experience of the real world, when they experience beauty, when they smell a rose, when they listen to the sea or smell a forest, they are experiencing something real. Though they deny its existence, they experience its reality.

This is their tension when they fall in love or when something greatly moves them. Their system may say, "There is no love." Yet their experience says, "I am in love." For a fleeting moment they have touched something. They have touched personality, they have felt love, they have experienced something absolute, something solid.

Everyone has enjoyed beauty. Everyone has experienced something that has moved them deeply inside. And when they do, they long for these things to convey meaning.

Yes, if I am a modern thinker I am in tension. On the basis of my presuppositions I say, "There are no absolutes. All is chance. There is no final and ultimate meaning." Yet within myself and in the universe I find that I experience meaning. The very facts of what I see and the very essence of what I am as a man contradict my own theory.

There are many examples of this inability to live consistently with modern assumptions. Francis Schaeffer states in *The God Who Is There* (p. 68) that John Cage, a well-known musician, produces his music totally by chance. He began composing by tossing coins, and later devised a mechanical conductor that worked in a wholly unpredictable way. He tried many things to produce pure chance sounds. And what resulted was noise, confusion, and silence.

Now Cage is also an outspoken believer in the universe-has-come-about-by-chance theory. His music reflects this. But he cannot live with his own conclusions. For one of John Cage's avid pastimes is collecting mushrooms. In fact, John Cage is now one of the leading amateur mushroom experts in the country and has compiled an extensive library on the subject. Though his view of the world is based on chance, he says, "I became aware that if I approached mushrooms in the spirit of my chance operations, I would die shortly. So I decided that I would not approach them in this way."

So here is a man trying to teach the world that the universe has come about by chance and yet he cannot even apply his own theory to picking mushrooms.

"Every truly modern man is forced to accept some sort of compromise in theory or practice, because the pressure of his own humanity demands it. He can say what he will concerning what he himself is, but no matter what he says he is, he is still a man" (Francis Schaeffer, *The God Who Is There,* p. 68).

4

Piecing the
Puzzle Together

Modern thinking seems to have led us right into a
morass. Let's begin to work our way out. Let's try
to find some answers. Not theories, but answers
we can consistently live with, that will fit the evidence we have observed in ourselves and in the
universe. We must look further at our presuppositions to decide which set of assumptions really
conforms to what exists. It is clear that most of us
have caught our presuppositions like we catch a
cold. We have automatically accepted much of the
relativism that our culture has forced upon us.

But as we observed earlier, though all society
may be saying "there are no absolutes," it is just
impossible to live consistently that way. We must
decide which presuppositions are really true. Not
just true for you or for me, but really true to what
is. We can't have it both ways; it just won't work.

So we must begin again, by means of presuppositions, to find what, if anything, is behind life, giving it meaning, if any. We are faced with two basic choices: absolutes either exist, or they do not.

There are a number of possible answers based on the assumption that final right, wrong, truth, and falsehood do not exist. From this presupposition spring a large number of religious answers which all have in common an impersonal beginning to the universe. Buddhism, Hinduism, pantheism, Life-Force philosophies, Unity, Reflection Church, Unification (and many others), all maintain a divine being of some sort exists, but say that it is not a personal being, above goodness and badness, and has little or no direct relations with man. Then there are answers which try to build potential explanations to the questions of life from man himself —such as modern science, rationalism, humanism, existentialism. All these theories are of course very different, but they share the idea of impersonality. And in the end they are reduced to no absolutes; stating that good, bad, truth, and falsehood are all ultimately equal. Whatever is behind the universe, they declare, is impersonal and therefore amoral.

The other possibility, if the presupposition is true that there are absolutes of right, wrong, truth, and falsehood is a personal view. Such a view detects a personal Being who made the universe. This is the Christian view which says there is a God who is good, who created the universe, and then created man and gave him instructions about how to live.

In looking at these two groups of possible answers, it would be ridiculous for us to say "they all teach basically the same thing." The impersonal explanations and personal Christianity differ at the foundational point of what God is like. Christianity says, "God is a person." The impersonal religions say He is not. He is not personal. He is not interested in you or me or good and bad. He is not even a "he." "It" is just there.

We've got to keep that in mind. It's easy to forget that "impersonal" really means impersonal. If you accept an impersonal supernatural being, it means you will never have any interaction with it. It is totally removed from man. It has no influence on us at all—good or bad. It is utterly beyond our reach, with no personality at all.

We also should mention another group of individuals who believe neither in an impersonal being nor in a personal God. You may be such a person. You don't really have a view on the supernatural at all. And you frankly don't care. You are living your life like you want to and are not too interested in "religious things." You might have some vague idea of belief, probably reflecting your childhood training, but it's not important to you anymore. You feel that as long as everyone does the best he can and stays out of everyone else's way, life will go along pretty smoothly.

Well, if that's what you believe, and if you've read this far, I imagine you can't help but see how the modern shift in the basic assumptions about absolutes has really drastically influenced your thinking. For without even knowing it, you have accepted the modern presupposition which denies absolutes.

For you say, "I'm trying to be good, but I don't

think everyone else has to be good in the same way I do. I don't believe in pushing my beliefs onto others."

And that statement is certainly one of the marks of the modern assumptions. Right and wrong are no longer absolute, but are relative to each individual.

So clearly, you do not actually fit between the personal and impersonal answers. On the basis of your assumptions about life, you have accepted the relative nature of truth and its impersonal implications.

Can It Be Put into Practice?

Now the one thing we must always keep in our minds when trying to find answers to these questions is this: whatever theory we choose must answer the evidence, and we must be able to live consistently with it. A theory that cannot be lived out in practice can't be true. It's as simple as that.

And as we have seen, the impersonal answer—no absolutes, no ultimate order or beauty, no personality, no love—is one that man simply cannot live out consistently. When you begin with the impersonal, eventually you are left with no final differences in life—between right and wrong or anything else.

And this is not how man lives. Man has morals and a conscience. Man has personality. And no matter how you word it, an impersonal beginning and subsequent chance developments simply cannot produce personality, morals, and conscience, meaning, order, beauty, or love. Darwin tried to account for these things, but wrote in his autobiography, "With my mind I cannot believe that these things come by chance" (From Francis Schaeffer, *The Church at the End of the Twentieth Century,* p. 15).

Francis Crick, the scientist who helped discover the meaning behind the DNA code, is another who says, "Man exists by chance. All has been chemically and physically determined beforehand. Man is but a machine."

But, Schaeffer points out (*He Is There and He is Not Silent.* Wheaton: Tyndale House, p. 2) that Crick is another modern thinker who cannot live on the basis of his own view. In one of his books in which he bases everything on the impersonal, he refers to nature as "she." He defines everything as impersonal, yet he suddenly gives personality to nature, which is behind it all. He cannot live with the implications of this impersonality. Man is simply unable to live consistently on the basis of impersonal chance.

So our problem continues. How can we find some explanation for this personality, this uniqueness, this rationality we find in ourselves? None of the impersonal religions or theories help. They say, "Personality doesn't exist." But we can't live by that statement. The impersonal answers just don't offer any explanation to what we see and feel.

Historic Christianity on the other hand, is based on absolutes and opposites. Right and wrong and truth and falsehood do exist, and are not ultimately just the same. They are different. Perhaps this personal answer, based on the long-held presupposition that absolutes do exist, bears a little more looking into.

Christianity holds that God, who has personality, and who is good, created the universe, and then created man. He created man "in His image," meaning He gave man personality and rationality. He set man apart in all His creation.

This begins to look promising. Could this be the explanation for all those unexplained things—morals, love of beauty, hope of meaning and significance—that make man unique? It seems so incredible that they could exist by chance. Christianity offers meaning for these things because of the very nature of the Christian God.

Francis Schaeffer says, "Christianity teaches the very reverse of what the Eastern thinker says. Man can understand and respond to the One who . . . made him and communicated with him . . . he was created to be different from the animal, the plant, and the machine" (*The God Who Is There,* p. 104).

The sharp contrast between Christianity and these other impersonal religions is hard for some to see. Many people want to be able to say, "Oh, yes, I believe in a God. But not a personal God." In so saying, they imagine they are elevating God to something "more than personal." But Christianity is the only religion to offer any idea of what a more-than-personal God could be like. All the other religions, though they might possibly say their god is more than personal, really think of him as something less, something impersonal. If you are looking for a God who is more than personal, suprapersonal, then you really are not faced with having to decide between the Christian idea and all the other religions. As the late English scholar, C. S. Lewis, said, "The Christian idea is the only one on the market" (*Mere Christianity*. New York: Macmillan Company, 1943, p. 125).

A Puzzle

We are now in the position of trying to fit together the pieces of a jigsaw puzzle. We have been given half the puzzle and have been trying to figure out the entire picture. What pieces do we have? What do we know?

Well, we know something about the universe and we know something about man. We know the universe has order and beauty and predictability. We know that man has reason, personality, morals, and love.

Several people have come along and said to us, "I have the missing pieces to your puzzle." How are we to know if they are indeed the right pieces that will make our picture complete? There is only one way. We must line up our half with the new pieces. If they line up, if the edges match, and if the picture is complete, then we have completed the puzzle. However, if the new pieces don't match, our only conclusion can be, "It doesn't match. It's a fraud!" The theories may have sounded good, but they didn't answer our most pressing question, "What about man and the universe? What about personality, order, meaning, and love?" They left our puzzle incomplete.

But then along came a man carrying a Bible,

who said, "The missing pieces to your puzzle are found in here." And when we examined the pieces more closely, we found God to be personal, we found He gave man personality and meaning and love and significance and morals. We found that God so placed man and the world together that both had meaning. Not relative meaning, but absolute meaning.

It begins to look promising. Maybe this is the genuine missing half to our puzzle. We would certainly never have guessed that the completed puzzle would look like this. But now that we have been told, it seems to fit in so well with all these things we already knew, I almost wonder we didn't guess it.

The Christian answer certainly seems to merit further examination.

5

A Consistent Answer

As long as modern man operates on the assumption of nonabsolutes, he never has to face the problem of evil in the world. After all, if everything is relative, then in the end good and evil are the same. So the existence of evil, suffering, and pain can be sidestepped.

However, once he looks more closely at the Christian answer, he is bound to ask, "If God really is good, in some absolute way, then why does so much pain and suffering exist? Why didn't He make everything good?"

"And what about that standard you were talking about?" he may add. "That thing always urging me to do right. You made it sound like that was a reason to believe Christianity. Yet it is clear I don't obey that standard most of the time. If Christianity teaches that absolute good and right exist, then why am I bad? Why is the world so messed up?"

These are tough questions. I'm sure you have asked them, as I have. And if Christianity holds any water at all, it should have an answer to them. Why is man both noble and meaningful, yet cruel? If a good standard exists, urging us to do right, then why do we not obey that urging? If God, supposedly good, has made us "in His image," then why does man seem to be so bad?

Any answer to the questions of life, any solution to our half-completed puzzle, must be able to deal with this or we must throw it out.

The impersonal answers we looked at deal with this problem of evil in a neat way. They simply say, "Evil doesn't exist" and that's the end of it. If there is any "something," any "being" behind it all, it is beyond good and evil—impersonal. In the end, therefore, the distinction between good and evil fades away.

It would be convenient if this were true. It would take care of a complex problem with a simple wave of the hand. But it's not that easy. Our experience tells us there are real differences between good and bad. Remember the standard we all feel? We behave as if good and bad really are different, no matter what our theory may say. This is clear evidence that the impersonal explanations do not complete the picture. They don't answer what we know about life. We can't live by what they teach.

Let's say, for example, that you and I were sitting in my living room. You were telling me that no real differences between good and bad exist. Now suppose I got up, walked over to the fireplace, picked up a flaming log, and set your hair alight. What would you do? Would you sit there calmly saying, "Good and evil are the same," while I set fire to your hair? Of course not. You see, it is impossible to live consistently on the basis of "all is ultimately equal." We just don't do it. We know it isn't true.

The Problem of Good and Evil

How does Christianity deal with the problem of good and evil? Many people through the years have tried to disclaim the worth of Christianity precisely at this point. Were they right? Does it in fact prove Christianity to be a fraud?

What do the Christians say about the existence of evil? In the beginning everything was good. God created worlds and beings and everything was good. Evil did not exist. But then something happened to change all that. One of God's created beings, Lucifer, the highest of all angels, rebelled. He tried to overthrow God. He failed, of course, so he was expelled from heaven, and began to wage a war against God which has lasted from that time until now. Lucifer managed to take a good many other angels with him. His forces increased, so this has indeed become a mighty warfare.

And according to the Christians, this is where evil came from. It was not in the universe originally, but it entered through Lucifer's rebellion against God. Once man entered the picture, the battle between good and evil became more intense. The struggle then moved from "the heavens" to man and his heart, his soul, and his actions. So from the beginning, man has always felt two things inside: promptings to obey the God who created him (good), and temptations to rebel against God (evil).

Christianity seems to meet the problem of evil head on. And from all we can see so far, its answer is consistent with what we know about ourselves. For you and I certainly do feel this tug-of-war going on inside us.

And in fact, it seems that this is the point where Christianity begins to make more sense than any other option we have looked at. For good and evil both have concrete origins and concrete reasons for being. Their existence can be logically explained. We don't have to get rid of them with a wave of the hand. And it seems that the whole conflict stems from the freedom God gave His created beings, man included. It would have been possible for Him to have created beings that had no power to rebel. But in so doing He would have apparently been eliminating the only joy or goodness worth having—the joy of freely choosing to love and obey.

God did not create evil, but evidently allowed for it by building into His creation the freedom to choose. It may not have been how you or I would have done it. But God apparently thought it worth the risk, and undoubtedly He was right. For how worthwhile would a world of automated, predetermined choices have been anyway?

So man, like the angels, was created perfectly good, in God's image. But he was also given this freedom to choose whether to obey. He was made so he could go either way—right or wrong. Evil therefore, though not created, became a possibility. And as man has chosen to disobey the principles of God throughout the years, evil in the world has resulted. God did not create it. In fact, He hates it. But in a certain sense, He must stand back and allow it to happen, to be consistent with the freedom He gave man in the first place.

Yet there is happiness for man too, in the midst of evil. The happiness God intended for His higher creatures (angels and men) is the happiness of choosing voluntarily to obey Him and be united with Him. So man has a choice. He can go either way. And he has.

That is the Christian explanation.

The fall of man seems to be the point on which all of Christianity turns. In explaining "Why is there bad if God is good?" the Christians say this state of affairs exists because things are not as they should be. "God's creation should be good," they say; "God created it that way. But the universe as it now stands is abnormal. It has changed. Man, as well as nature, is now, in a sense, separated from God."

So the bad exists because all the universe is not united with God, who is good, as it was to begin with. Man separated himself from God, by choice, by allying himself with the fallen angels and disobeying God's instructions. The Christians have a word for this imperfect state of separation. They call it sin.

The word "sin" probably expresses one of the most misunderstood concepts in all of Christianity.

For many years whenever I heard the word "sin" I immediately thought "bad." And that is, I suppose, true of most of us. But actually that is not what the word means at all.

Sin simply describes our state of being—separated from God. Sin describes the abnormal state of affairs in the universe.

Our goodness or badness and our daily activities (some good and some bad) are not what sin is. But our daily bad actions do serve as a reminder that this state of separation does indeed exist between ourselves and God. If we were not separated from God, we would be good. But we find ourselves being bad. This continually shows us that we are indeed separated from God.

This is why so many people confuse sin with what we do. They think the wrong we commit is the sin. But the badness is only a reminder that sin (separation) exists. The badness is a barometer, an indicator. The fall of the barometer is not the storm. It only indicates the storm is coming. Our badness is the same way. It is not the sin, but it indicates the sin is there. And the sin then explains why we are bad, just as the storm explains why the needle of the barometer dropped. Sin is not being bad, it is being separated.

So when Christians say, "Turn from sin," they are not saying "Quit being bad."

They are simply saying, "Unite yourself with God. Bridge the gap."

And this makes sense. For it would be impossible to become good if our natures were inherently bad. That would be hardly within our power. But if sin is really just a state—a position, a separation—then quite possibly it could be overcome.

Let's look further. Let's see if this is possible.

Well, Christians not only say man is separated from God. They say he shouldn't be. They say that even though we are part of this gigantic rebellion that has been going on since the day Lucifer rebelled, we still bear the image of God. There is still a part of us that is "Godlike." This is the standard we were talking about. Maybe it could be called conscience, or something else. But in each of us there is something higher, something nobler, something which longs for good. We have all seen this at work in ourselves. We have felt love, we have felt compassion, we have longed for meaning. All these things are tiny instances of that peculiar something found in every man. And Christians say this is the "image of God" showing through. Showing through even in our separated condition.

This is why the Christian message apparently is simple. It seems we only hear two things, "God loves you. Turn from sin." We see that Christianity really has no other message. This is the whole of it. We must be reminded of our separated condition ("Turn from sin"). This sin has no degrees because it is not what we *do* at all. It is what we are and where we are. And though some men are worse than others, we are all equally separated from God. That is our sin.

But then the Christians say, "God loves you." The other half of their message is, "Though we are separated from Him, we still bear God's image. We are still meaningful. He still loves us. He can bring us again into the fellowship with Him which He created us to enjoy. He can overcome the sin. He can eliminate the separation."

At this point we don't really know how this is to be done. But we already see answers here that none of the other religions provide. Nothing else explains this abnormality we see in the universe. Nothing else explains this dual nature we see in ourselves—good and bad. But Christianity says it is the natural state of a good man gone sour. Christianity explains why our behavior is not what it ought to be and it explains why we all feel a longing to be better. Christianity gives meaning to our personality and rationality, and especially to our love. They don't have to be explained away. If Christianity is true, they reflect the God who made us. Even though we are part of a rebellion against Him, our very natures still reflect Him. The universe, though part of the Fall, the rebellion, still reflects God. Therefore it has meaning, beauty, and significance. C. S. Lewis called the earth "enemy-occupied territory" (*Mere Christianity*, p. 36), and maintained that this is where we find the Christian solution to man's dilemma of being pulled two ways at once. God has landed in this enemy-occupied territory in human form. This is the point where Christianity becomes totally unique in all the religions of the world. For Christianity says that God became man.

It Works!
Now exactly how this happened is not clear. And exactly why this specific means was necessary, and

why it worked to bridge the separation that existed, is not clear either. Of course, libraries have been written to try to explain these things. But the point Christianity makes is, "Though it cannot be completely explained, it works." God's becoming a man, His submission to death at the hands of the very men He made, His conquering death and coming back to life, His sending His Spirit to live in men, these things overcome the separation (sin) that existed. They make possible a reinstatement of our original fellowship with God.

This is the whole story the Bible is trying to tell. God chose this method as a means to solve the problem of sin, and we could invent many theories for the how and why of it. But the point Christians make is that it works! Jesus' dying disabled death itself, and makes possible a relationship with God that He intended us to have when He created us. This is not easy to understand. In fact, it is probably impossible to understand. Theories have been advanced. But the theories are not Christianity; they are only attempts to explain something which cannot be explained. The important thing is that it works.

C. S. Lewis pointed out in his book, *Mere Christianity* (p. 43), that if you are hungry and tired, a warm meal will do you good. But when you sit down to eat it, you are not thinking about vitamins, protein, carbohydrates, and how they work. People ate their dinners and were strengthened and refreshed long before anyone ever heard of vitamins and proteins. And if sometime in the future a new theory is adopted about how our bodies use food, we will all go on eating our dinners just the same. And the food will continue to do its work, whether we understand it or not.

In the same way, a man can accept what Jesus has done without knowing anything about how it works. We are told that Jesus died for us and that His death overcame our sin, our separation from God. That is the formula. Further attempts to explain it are secondary to the fact that it works.

Death Gives Life

Should it really surprise us that Christ's death should be that on which the fate of mankind depends? Don't we observe that death itself often gives life? Isn't it in fact one of the laws of nature we see about us all the time? The changing seasons remind us of the constant theme: life—death—life. Every growing thing on the earth exists because somewhere, at some time, a small seed died, and from it new life came forth.

A man and woman give their lives sacrificially for their child. And in the end they die, but he lives on. Something about Jesus dying that we might live rings true to what we know about the rest of existence. How significant His simple statement becomes, "Unless a grain of wheat falls into the earth and dies, it remains by itself alone; but if it dies, it bears much fruit" (John 12:24, NASB).

"The Christian system is consistent as no other system that has ever been . . . it has that quality that no other system completely has—you begin at the beginning, and you go to the end. It is as simple as that . . . Our generation longs for the reality of personality but it cannot find it. But Christianity says personality is valid because personality is rooted in the personal God who has always been" (Francis Schaeffer, *The God Who Is There*, p. 156).

"If Christianity does turn out to be true," you may wonder, "then what about all those other religions? Are they wrong? How could so many millions of people be deceived? Mustn't there be some truth in those religions too?"

Yes, I think you're right. There is some truth in even the most obscure and unusual of the world's religions. At least some hint of it. If you are an atheist, you have to persuade yourself that most of the rest of the human race has always been wrong on the one single question that matters most. However, if you are a Christian you can take a more liberal view. The life and teachings, death and resurrection of Jesus do not necessarily deny all the other world religions; in fact they fulfill many of them. Until Jesus came, all the other religious attempts of man through the years were incomplete. Once Jesus came to reveal the complete truth about man's relationship with God, the other religions became obsolete.

But of course a Christian believes that where Christianity differs from other religions, Christianity is right and they are wrong. It is just like an arithmetic problem. There is only one right answer. But some of the wrong answers are nearer being right than others.

One final thing that sets Christianity apart from all other world religions is the historical and physical evidence for its truth. Not only is Christianity consistent, it is realistic. Christians do not say, "Accept it blindly." They base their claim for its truth on facts: the state of the universe, the state of man, the historically documented life and death of Jesus, and the happenings among His followers ever since.

In that sense it is almost a nonreligious religion. Francis Schaeffer points out that when Paul, for instance, "was asked whether Jesus was raised from the dead, he gave a completely nonreligious answer in the 20th century sense: 'There are almost five hundred living witnesses; go and ask them'" (*The God Who Is There*, p. 65).

Schaeffer says that Christianity "is prepared to face the consequences of being proved false, and say with Paul, 'If you find the body of Christ, the discussion is finished, let us eat and drink for tomorrow we die'" (*The God Who Is There*, p. 46).

But the body has never been found. And on the solid historical evidence of the resurrection, Christianity stands alone among the religions of the world.

6

Does Consistency Matter?

We have looked at the changes in thinking that have taken place and which have influenced us. We have seen some of the inconsistencies that arise when we try to put these new ways of thinking into practice. We looked at several "religious" ways of explaining these inconsistencies. We have tried to find some theory that would both fit our observations about the universe and ourselves. We have seen that theories based on an impersonal supernatural simply do not work. It is impossible to live consistently according to what they teach.

As we examined the Christian answer, we saw that it did in fact logically deal with and answer our questions about man and the universe, as well as the problem of evil in the world.

One final question remains. Is it possible to live consistently on the basis of the Christian answer? If so, our search is ended.

But first we must ask an even more basic question. Does living consistently even matter? What does it mean to be consistent?

Remember that presuppositions are those basic assumptions about life we all have and that we take for granted. Everyone has his own set of presuppositions that are the basis for his beliefs. The only way to really know if a presupposition is valid or not is to extend it to its logical conclusion.

Once you accept nonabsolute, impersonal, chance presuppositions as the basis for your life, it is impossible to be logically consistent to them. The reason is, simply, because we must live in the reality of the world and with ourselves; and in the world and in man there is massive evidence of personality, meaning, and absolutes. So there is tension between a man's incorrect presuppositions and his life in the real world. The more logical a man is to his incorrect presuppositions the further away from the real world he is.

Such a man, if his presuppositions are wrong, lives somewhere between the real world and the logical conclusions of his ideas. Most people have never analyzed this, and so live illogically and inconsistently without giving it a thought. But there always exists some point of inconsistency. Every person who has accepted nonabsolute, impersonal answers stands in a position he cannot logically pursue to the end.

There are numerous examples of this point of inconsistency. The French existentialists Camus and Sartre exhibited it. They both held that there were no absolute answers, that the universe was meaningless, that no God existed, that morals and hope and all values had no meaning. But neither of them could live consistently with this.

Camus never gave up hope in his search for moral meaning. He denied the existence of morals, yet continued to look for them.

Sartre also denied the existence of any morals or lasting value or difference between right and wrong. But then he took a moral position. He signed a political document, the Algerian Manifesto. He, too, could not consistently carry out his position (*The God Who Is There*, p. 123).

The famous painter, Picasso, also demonstrated this. His abstract paintings show the loss of form and order and absolutes and meaning. He was truly a modern thinker. He would have said in effect, "Love does not exist; meaning does not exist; there are no ultimate values."

But then one day Picasso fell in love. And across his next painting were sprawled the words, "I love Eva." His presuppositional position denied that love even existed. But his manhood could not live with this (*The God Who Is There*, p. 32).

John Cage, the composer, once directed the New York Philharmonic Orchestra playing some of his own chance music. When it was over and he was taking his bows, he thought he heard a leak from the steam pipes. He heard hissing. But then he realized that the audience was hissing *him*—they did not like the music.

But the ironic thing is that many of those in the audience really believed philosophically exactly as John Cage did—that the universe is based on the impersonal and has come about by chance. But when faced with the logical result of such an assumption—chance music—they revolted. They did not like it.

But what were they really doing? They were hissing themselves (*The Church at the End of the Twentieth Century*, p. 22).

The recent Watergate scandal in the United States has caused the same reaction. The Nixon administration acted on the suppositions actually held by a large part of the country—a loss of moral values, a loss of absolutes. And once the lid was blown off, it seemed the whole country turned on a handful of men and said, "You men lied. You broke the law and betrayed our trust."

But that same administration had been elected by the people of the country twice. How could we pin the entire blame on them? And most people in this country hold to moral absolutes no more than those indicted. But still we are quick to point our fingers and say, "You . . . You . . . You. . ."

But like the hissing audience, we are pointing our fingers at ourselves. For the Nixon administration only demonstrated the logical results of what many in the country really believe. The real inconsistency lies with those of us who have turned on Nixon and his men but are actually living according to the same presuppositions ourselves.

Does Living Consistently Mean Living Perfectly?

These examples drive us once again back to the question, "Does consistency matter?" It is certainly clear that many people live inconsistently, being illogical to their own assumptions and beliefs. But what does this tell us of such a man and his point of view? What does it tell us of his assumptions and beliefs about life?

Certainly, if a man is holding an idea that cannot be lived out in practice it does not speak well of his theory. The scientist adopts a theory and then asks, "Does it work?" We must do the same. "Does it work?" must be our guideline. If Sartre's theory, and Camus' and Piscasso's cannot be logically held by these very men, we do well to disregard their teaching.

Of course, consistency is of no consequence to the man who is unconcerned with truth at all. If you don't care whether your life has meaning or not, then why bother worrying about consistency?

But for the man who wants to practice truth, and wants to have a basis for being able to say things about life, there must be consistency. Any person who wants to live honestly, logically, and truthfully must be consistent with his beliefs. If he isn't, we have no reason to listen to what he has to say.

And now we encounter another of the unique aspects of Christianity. For when we look at Christians who have been practicing their faith a long time (not just talking about it) we see a logical consistency almost unknown today. When you ask them about their beliefs, they are the first to say, "As Christians, living consistently certainly doesn't mean living perfectly."

They explain further. "This world is abnormal. We will never be able to live perfectly in this life.

But as Christians, we have a plan for improvement. Growth is the key to the Christian life."

So it seems that the flaws we all notice in Christians are not signs that Christianity is untrue. In fact, it is just the opposite. Imperfect Christians are what Christianity (with its plan for improvement) is all about. Christianity seems to be a system that has the flaws, mistakes, failings, and stumblings of the individual built right into it: they are part of the process.

If you are a Christian, you must accept the world as an imperfect place and yourself as an imperfect being right at the start. That is where a consistent life begins. Then you allow God to affect your life from day to day so that you slowly grow toward the sort of life that Jesus demonstrated. Of course, you will not arrive at that life before death. There will be many setbacks, but there will also be progress. And over many years you will begin to manifest the characteristics He showed in His life.

7

The Cost
of Consistency

If consistent Christian living begins with accepting yourself and the world as imperfect, where does it go from there? It must surely mean more than just assenting to the Christian doctrines and saying, "Yes, I believe those are true." For we have seen that many people accept other doctrines, yet aren't able to conform to them in practice. Saying, "I believe" doesn't necessarily mean a thing.

There are people throughout the Western world who consider themselves Christians simply because they generally accept the Christian ethic of being good. There are many who know the facts of Christianity (Jesus' life and teachings) and believe them. They may even be regular churchgoers and Bible readers. To you or me they may seem very religious, very Christian.

But are they? Again the crucial question. What *exactly* is consistent Christian living?

To find an answer, I think we should look closely at the word "believe." To you and me today, belief is usually an opinion. If you are persuaded something is true, you say, "I believe that is true."

If we are discussing New Testament authorship, you may remark, "I *believe* the Book of Hebrews was written by Barnabas." That is how we use the word. So I ask you, "Do you believe Christianity is true?" And you might answer, "Yes, I believe it. I am persuaded it is true." Then I ask, "Are you a Christian?"

It is clear that in your opinion the tenets of Christianity are true. You think that when lined up alongside the other world religions, only Christianity gives adequate answers. You believe the accounts of Jesus' life, and that He died and came back to life. You realize His death was in some way for you, so that you might have fellowship with God. You believe the Bible is true, and you may go to church. Are you a Christian?

What Does It Mean To Believe?

We must look even closer at the word "believe." Jesus repeatedly called His listeners to believe. The message of belief is on nearly every page of the Bible. What is meant by it?

Well, as I investigated this word, I discovered something very interesting. I found that for most of my life I had quite misunderstood its meaning. For I found that believe, as used in the Bible and by Jesus, is much different from our normal use of the word. It does *not* mean to hold an opinion. Let me quote from the original *Webster's Dic-*

tionary: "The primary sense of believe is to throw or put to, or to assent to; to leave with or to rest on; to rely. . . . To believe on is to trust, to place full confidence in, to rest upon with faith."

Evidently belief has more to do with our actions than our opinions. And this is precisely how Jesus used the word. When He said, "Believe in Me," He meant far more than simply agreeing that He existed. It must be so, because to His listeners standing there with Him, the statement, "Be sure that I exist and am really here" would have been ridiculous. How could they have thought otherwise? He was standing right there in front of them.

Surely He must have meant more. And looking at the rest of His teachings, we see that in fact He meant to trust, rely on, rest on, submit to, obey, and love Him—to turn over every area of life to Him. Belief entailed the full scope of life, not merely opinions. In fact, as Jesus used it, belief led the early Christians into complete submission to Jesus, and often to death. Belief was a total way of life.

Again Webster says, "The word implies, with this assent of mind, a yielding of the will and affections."

So after my study of this word, I had no choice but to conclude that the Christian is not necessarily the person who simply holds that Christianity (as a set of ideas) is true. The Christian must be the person who is trusting, depending on, and submitting to Jesus in a moment-by-moment way. It is the person whose goal in life is to live the life Jesus demonstrated and taught. Of course, this says nothing about life-style. The life of Jesus can be lived by a student, an executive, a housewife, a child, a millionaire, a president, a professor, a carpenter, or a clerk. The life of Jesus is the life of behaving toward others as Jesus taught us. And that means more than just being nice. It is a total life-style, as taught in the New Testament.

Though I may have studied these things and presented them to you; and though you may have followed every detail and believed them all—that would not make either one of us a Christian. A mere agreement that these things are true is not a true "belief" in Christianity. Jesus came, bringing a new life-style, not a new world religion. Christianity isn't something we talk about. It is something we do. The only reason I have been talking about it is so we both can get on with the business of doing it. Neither one of us can say, "I believe," unless we are willing to go the whole route and believe as He meant it. There is simply no other way.

That is why we can't become Christians without submitting to a complete change in our lives. What we often want to say is, "I don't expect to be a saint. All I want is to be an ordinary decent fellow." And we mistake this for humility. But this is our fatal error. Naturally we never expected to be made into the sort of men He intends to make us into. We never asked to be either. But the question is no longer what we intended at all. Once we take the first step toward belief, the question becomes, "What did He intend for us when He made us?"

So it is difficult—no, impossible—to go part way

with Christianity. C. S. Lewis has compared it with a visit to the dentist (*Mere Christianity*, p. 157). When you were a child you may have had a toothache. You knew that if you went to your mother she would find something to give you that would ease the pain for the night. But you didn't go to your mother if you could help it. And the reason was this: you knew she would give you the aspirin, but you also knew she would take you to see the dentist the following morning. It was impossible for you to get what you wanted from her without getting something more that you did not want. All you wanted was for the pain to go away. But of course, your mother knew that could never happen until you got your teeth attended to. And the dentist was the same way. He would even fiddle around with other teeth that weren't even hurting yet. He just wouldn't let them be. If you gave him the opportunity, he would try to fix every tooth.

Now if the analogy will hold up, God is like the dentist. If you give Him an inch He will take a mile. Thousands of people go to Him, thinking He will cure them of one particularly annoying vice. But He doesn't stop there, even though that may be all you asked for. Once you open up and call Him in, you will get the full treatment.

No wonder then that Jesus warned His listeners to "count the cost" before following Him. "Make no mistake," He said, "I will make you perfect if you give Me half the chance. If you put yourself in My hands, you are in for nothing less. You can still choose to push Me away. But if you do not, if you do choose to have Me, understand that I will see it through. No matter what suffering it may cost you now, and what purification it may even cost you after death, and no matter what it costs Me, I will not rest until you are perfect. My Father must be able to look at you and say He is well pleased with you, just as He did to Me. This is where we are going if you throw in with Me. Count the cost, because I can make you perfect. I can and I will. And I will certainly not do anything less."

Therefore we cannot be a Christian, but then only go half way. It is impossible to say "It is true" and do nothing more. To be a Christian we must willingly accept and submit to all that God has for us.

C. S. Lewis said, "The Christian way is different; harder and easier. Christ says, 'Give Me all. I don't want so much of your time and so much of your money and so much of your work; I want you. I have not come to torment your natural self, but to kill it. No half-measures are any good. I don't want to cut off a branch here and a branch there, I want to have the whole tree down. I don't want to drill the tooth, or crown it, or stop it, but to have it out. Hand over the whole natural self, all the desires which you think innocent as well as the ones you think wicked—the whole outfit. I will give you a new self instead. In fact, I will give you Myself; My own will shall become yours'" (*Mere Christianity*, p. 153).

That is the impossible, terrible thing about following Jesus—handing over everything. Your whole self. And yet, impossible as it seems, it turns out to be easier than what we are trying to do instead. For we are all trying to keep hold of ourselves and all of our selfish desires, and at the same time be "good" in some spiritual way. We are trying to behave as "Christians" while letting our hearts and minds and motives go their own way. C. S. Lewis then continued, "And that is exactly what Christ warned us you could not do. As He said, 'a thistle cannot produce figs.' If I am a field that contains nothing but grass-seed, I cannot produce wheat. Cutting the grass may keep it short; but I shall still produce grass and no wheat. If I want to produce wheat, the change must go deeper than the surface, I must be ploughed up and re-sown" (*Mere Christianity*, p. 154).

So the Christian life is not something we can "put on" over our old life. The Christian life is a new life. The changes must go all the way down. And yet making those changes is not primarily our responsibility. It is His. Once we take the first step, He will see that the new life spreads through us. It will come slowly at first. But in making our first feeble efforts, and in letting Him work on the parts of us He chooses, the changes will happen.

"He never talked vague idealistic gas. When He said 'be perfect,' He meant it. He meant that we must go in for the full treatment. It is hard; but the sort of compromise we are all hankering after is harder—in fact, it is impossible. It may be hard for an egg to turn into a bird; it would be a jolly sight harder for it to learn to fly while remaining an egg. We are like eggs at present. And you cannot go on indefinitely being just an ordinary, decent egg. We must be hatched or go bad. . . . This is the whole of Christianity. There is nothing else" (C. S. Lewis, *Mere Christianity*, pp. 154-155).

8

Real Things
Are Not Simple

If you're still standing on the outside peering in, one of the supreme difficulties about Christianity results from Jesus' statement, "Unless you are converted and become like children, you shall not enter the kingdom of heaven" (Matt. 18:3, NASB). This stresses the simplicity of Christianity.

Many Christians are guilty of mistaking this statement to seem to mean that if you are good it doesn't matter if you are an ignoramus. But they are wrong. Christ wants the heart of a child, but the intellect of a mature adult. He wants our intelligence alert and sharp. That is why He told us to be "shrewd as serpents, and innocent as doves" (Matt. 10:16, NASB).

Many non-Christians, anxious to blow holes in the credibility of Christianity, take these words of simplicity and read no further. They invent a version of the Christian faith hardly suitable for a young child, and then make that the object of their criticism. But if you try to explain some of the basic doctrines of Christianity to them in a mature and instructive fashion, they then complain that you are making it too complicated. There is no use even talking with someone who is going to change his ground every several minutes and whose goal is to discredit Christianity.

If we're to be honest in this search, we can't allow ourselves to be guilty of either of these two errors. Christianity in its totality is simple, yet profound and often difficult. It cannot be grasped in one sitting. But simple religions are rare. Simple things are rare. Many things look simple but are not. Apples growing on a tree look simple enough. But if you were to ask me to explain how they got there, that would be more difficult. It would require a detailed yet clear explanation.

So real things are not simple; they are often complicated, and are frequently odd. They are not precise and neat, as you would have expected. As C. S. Lewis once commented, when we're first taught that the earth and other planets go around the sun, our first thought is that the solar system must be orderly. The planets must somehow match and possibly be evenly distant from the sun, or at least spaced at predictable intervals. There should be some pattern to their size and behavior. You'd naturally expect them to travel in circles around the sun. But in fact, you find no rhyme or reason to it at all. They are odd sizes, spaced at varying distances, made up of vastly different substances and atmospheres. They don't travel in circles, some have a moon, others have none, one has four, and one has a ring.

We could never have guessed this arrangement. And so it is with much of reality. We'd never guess it. C. S. Lewis concludes, "This is one of the reasons I believe Christianity. It is a religion you could not have guessed. If it offered us just the kind of universe we had always expected, I should feel we were making it up. But, in fact, it is not the sort of thing anyone would have made up. It has just that queer twist about it that real things have. So let us leave behind all these boys philosophies—these over-simple answers. The problem is not simple and the answer is not going to be simple either" (*Mere Christianity*, pp. 32-33).

Christianity is not neat and simple. There are no ready-made formulas. If God has revealed truth to us about our existence, this truth is often complex. We must reason it out logically, like mature, thinking adults. And then once we have discovered it to indeed be true, we must simply yield to God on the basis of who He is and what He has done. Nothing else need be said. We owe God everything we are, simply because He is God.

And this is the discomfort of it all. This is the point where so many of us turn and walk away from all that God has to offer us. We have been brought up thinking that we are our own masters. Submission to another runs contrary to all we have been taught and all we feel. This is our problem. We are rebels at heart. Even though our self contains no lasting life to give us, no happiness, no joy, still we cling to it. We refuse to submit. We refuse to bow before God. As Schaeffer put it, "'Men turn away not because what is said makes no sense, but because they do not want to bow before the God who is there" (*The God Who Is There*, p. 102). But in our refusal, we hold to something which will never succeed in giving us the life we're looking for.

"The reason why it can never succeed is this. God made us; invented us as a man invents a machine. A car is made to run on gasoline, and it would not run properly on anything else. Now God designed the human machine to run on Himself. He Himself is the fuel our spirits were designed to burn, or the food our spirits were designed to feed on. There is no other. That is why it is just no good asking God to make us happy in our own way without bothering about religion. God cannot give us happiness and peace apart from Himself, because it is not there. There is no such thing" (C. S. Lewis, *Mere Christianity*, p. 39).

We cannot come to Him because of what we are going to receive. But when we do come to Him for the right reasons, everything else will be added besides (peace, joy, difficulties, eternal life, meaning, and true personality). "Until you have given up yourself to Him you will not have a real self . . . The principle runs through all life from top to bottom. Give up your self, and you will find your real self. Lose your life and you will save it. Submit to death, death of your ambitions and favorite wishes every day and the death of your whole body in the end; submit with every fibre of your being, and you will find eternal life. Keep back nothing. Nothing that you have not given away will ever really be yours. Nothing in you that has not died will ever be raised from the dead. Look for yourself, and you will find in the long run only hatred, loneliness, despair, rage, ruin, and decay. But look for Christ and you will find Him, and with Him everything else thrown in" (C. S. Lewis, *Mere Christianity,* p. 175).

Appendix 1

Great Moral Teacher?

Reactions to the man Jesus are very diverse, and often interesting. One recent development in the long history of man's response to Him is the "great moral teacher" response. Jesus was a good man, a great moral teacher whose teachings have done the world much good. However, He was just a man after all.

Here is C. S. Lewis' reply to that interpretation:

Christ says that He is "humble and meek" and we believe Him; not noticing that, if He were merely a man, humility and meekness are the very last characteristics we could attribute to some of His sayings.

I am here trying to prevent anyone saying the really foolish thing that people often say about Him: "I am ready to accept Jesus as a great moral teacher, but I don't accept His claim to be God." That is the one thing we must not say. A man who was merely a man and said the sort of things Jesus said would not be a great moral teacher. He would either be a lunatic—on a level with the man who says he is a poached egg—or else he would be the Devil of Hell. You must make your choice. Either this man was, and is, the Son of God; or else a madman or something worse. You can shut Him up for a fool, you can spit at Him and kill Him as a demon; or you can fall at His feet and call Him Lord and God. But let us not come with any patronising nonsense about His being a great human teacher. He has not left that open to us. He did not intend to (*Mere Christianity*, p. 41).

Appendix 2

Consistency versus Consistency

My repeated use of the word "consistent" could possibly create a misunderstanding that I would like to dispel. There can be two kinds of consistency or inconsistency associated with the things we have been talking about: consistency of a system or a religion or a doctrine; and consistency of an individual. In this book we have been using the word to refer to the consistency of various systems. Our purpose has been to examine the validity of doctrinal systems the world has to offer.

Now granted, we did talk about individuals. But only in order to discover some things about their systems. The inconsistencies we noted were inherent in the systems, not the individuals.

We have been examining different world views from the outside. We have been trying to decide where truth is. Once that decision is made, we then must move into that system. But when we move inside, consistency then becomes an altogether different thing. From inside Christianity, you and I can look at inconsistency or hypocrisy, both in ourselves and in others, and deal with it and try to overcome it. But that cannot happen until we actually come inside; until after the question has been settled with all the other potential systems.

If I say, "I am inconsistent. I cannot faithfully live the life of Jesus," you must realize I am speaking from the inside. I am speaking to "my own," to the family of Christians who understand what I mean. And we all must make this admission, because it is true.

But from the outside, as I stand comparing Christianity with many other possible answers to the dilemmas of man, I can say, "Christianity is consistent like no other system. I can live consistently as a Christian." And here I am using the word in a completely different sense. Here I am talking about the feasibility of Christianity when pitted against the problems of man. But from inside, once that initial question has been settled, my talk of consistency is almost an introspective thing, part of what I must face in my "plan for improvement."

A key difference between Christianity and other philosophical systems is that the others all depend on what man does, while Christianity comes out and states at the beginning that man can accomplish *nothing* for himself, no matter what he does. Christianity as a system depends solely on what God does. On that basis, it can be flawlessly consistent even while dealing day by day with our seemingly infinite human inconsistencies.

In one sense, therefore, you do have the right to judge Christianity on the basis of what I as a Christian am like. But in another sense you do not. You can say, "If Christianity is true, then surely it should make a difference in his life. There should be a change. He should be nicer and kinder and gentler than before." That you can say. And that you should say.

As C. S. Lewis has clarified, you cannot say, "Christian Clarence should be nicer and kinder and gentler than non-Christian Ralph" (*Mere Christianity*, p. 164). For comparisons of this sort are no good. Ralph may be a pleasant sort of guy all on his own and Clarence may have a kidney disorder that gives him a bad temper. Their raw material might be quite different. All you can ask is, "Has being a Christian improved Clarence's temper?" or "How much nicer might Ralph be if he were a Christian?"

So in evaluating Christianity, don't make the fatal error of disregarding it because some particular Christian you know seems to you a hypocrite. If you do, you're mistakenly judging Christianity from the outside by a judgment that can only be made from the inside. Shortcomings in individual Christians are very common, very natural, and even very necessary. But until you come all the way inside the Christian faith, you have no way of properly evaluating these shortcomings and seeing them in their real perspective.

Appendix 3

After the Decision, Then What?

I would like to remind you what my purpose has been. I have simply tried to clarify some of the crucial issues to help you decide whether or not Christianity is true. This has not been a description of what Christianity is, how to become a growing Christian, Christian doctrine, or what the Bible says. This has merely been a look about us to see that Christianity is confirmed by what we see and who we are. For more detail about Christianity itself you will have to go to other sources such as the Bible, books, and Christian people. I take the words of Jesus seriously when He said, "count the cost." Being a Christian is a serious business. Once you take the step it will take every bit of you.

However, you may have been reading this and found it all made sense. You may feel Christianity is exactly what you want. And now you have even more unanswered questions than before. All kinds of things are coming to your mind that I didn't even mention: How do you become a Christian? What do you do then? How does God's plan for improvement work? What about church?

If you find yourself in this boat, I'd like to make some brief suggestions to help you get started. First, find a good Christian bookstore. Get a recent translation of the Bible and read the Gospels and then the New Testament. They will be your guidelines. There you will find how a Christian is to live.

Also, buy a copy of C. S. Lewis' *Mere Christianity* and read it over three or four times. If you are interested in further discussion about modern thinking versus Christianity, read some of Francis Schaeffer's books. He goes into much more detail than I did here.

Then begin to get to know your Christian bookstore. Browse. Read some biographies about Christian people:

Brother Andrew, et al. *God's Smuggler*. Old Tappan, New Jersey: Fleming H. Revell Co., 1968.

Colson, Charles. *Born Again*. Old Tappan, New Jersey: Fleming H. Revell Co., 1976.

Grubb, Norman P. *Rees Howells: Intercessor*. Fort Washington, Pennsylvania: Christian Literature Crusade, Inc., 1964-1967.

Lewis, C. S. *Surprised by Joy: The Shape of My Early Life*. New York: Harcourt Brace Jovanovich, Inc., 1966.

Schaeffer, Edith. *L'Abri*. Wheaton, Illinois: Tyndale House Publishers, 1969.

ten Boom, Corrie, et al. *The Hiding Place*. Old Tappan, New Jersey: Fleming H. Revell Co., 1974.

Wilkerson, David. *The Cross and the Switchblade*. Old Tappan, New Jersey: Fleming H. Revell Co.

Get a book on studying the Bible and use it. Investigate books on prayer. In short, begin to learn and grow as a Christian. On the shelves of your Christian bookstore are the greatest teachers you will ever meet. Learn from them.

Seek out Christians. Talk to them, ask them questions, pray with them, learn from them. As a new Christian, you can't grow in a cocoon. You must interact with people.

Most importantly, as you begin to learn about the kind of life you are supposed to live as a Christian, *do it!* If you don't practice it, that life will eventually wither and die. Living the Christian life isn't automatic. You must cultivate it. That is the key to life as a Christian.